one thousand matches

carly macisaac

Cover Design by Suhaila Baheyeldin

my dear readers,

you are salt water and sunlight

you are the moon, in all its phases

you are electric.

I painted it yellow

Of fear you'd see how tangled and black I really was

That my true form may be seeping through

My nerve damage showing

Inhale

allowing the harsh smoke to bite into my lungs

and escape from my lips.

Cool summer air

tiny droplets of rain on my bare shoulders

the heartbeat of this concrete jungle.

I miss everyone I've ever known, all at once

and wonder how your love gets so stuck.

I wash you down with another drink

hoping the blur of the city lights will close the gap

that your absence has sewn into my skin.

"tell me something that makes you feel naked"

he said

undressing me with his eyes

if I revealed that

would you be relieved or terrified

that your demons matched mine?

3

my freckles were flustered when they heard you call us beautiful

but a lump in the back of my throat started to rise
how can it be possible to feel so completely flattered
and so completely misunderstood
all at the same time

is beautiful all we get to be?

drained lungs

tangled curls

sweaty palms

crooked smile

hollow laugh

tingling toes

this was the shell of myself he liked best.

he saw my bare soul
the core of who i was

and he left

A dark cloud hung over us that day. I resented you for doing that,
for spoiling all the moments that mattered.
It was just like you to find a way to leak through the cracks
like a seeping needy blood stain that appears suddenly,
on a perfectly white shirt.

The grip of loneliness wrapped its icy fingers around my throat
suffocating my sounds
muzzling all the chaos in my mind.
It was a freezer-burn kind of numbness,
and that's the way I liked it.

In the wake, the stillness /
my bones ached for your fingertips
to trace the shadows of my skin again
to have your limbs entangled up in mine

You were stitched in my veins and you knew it
But I could always taste the goodbye on your tongue /

as a child

in my Five Star notebook

hidden deep within the perfect blue lines

I wrote down the compliments I received from people who meant something to me

mostly from my grade school teachers, or my grandfather

I didn't tell anyone

but when I felt insignificant

I would trace my fingers over the words,

reminding myself I might one day believe them.

I ripped it

You're gonna break it

Let me do it

It shattered

why can't she hear me when I speak? i ask myself this often.
she has this horribly annoying habit of becoming emotionally
vacant the exact moment i need her most. it makes my head
explode. sometimes i can actually feel my eyes rolling out of
my head. i imagine them rolling around on the car floor as
she shrieks, slamming on the breaks.

I own a conflicting desire
to be seen and hidden
at the exact same moment in time.

I am a collector of broken people
I line them up, high upon the shelves
like porcelain Antoinette dolls
dust off cobwebs
straighten corsets with nimble fingers
shine shoes with the blouse off my back

Their pain becomes my pain
as they paint their traumas onto the windowsill of my soul
Hang their hats on my "Are you okay?"s and "I'm here to listen"s
the weight of the world a balancing act now relying on my bruised and shaky legs

the empathic tendencies that extend from my mouth and land into greedy, sweaty palms
have become a full-time job I don't remember applying for

I am a collector of broken people
my heart another prop displayed in the storefront of my remorse
open 24/7 but rarely for sale.

find
someone
who
does
not
view
their
commitment
to
you
as
a
weight

when I think about that theatre I remember how it felt
to have my guts trickling out of me every night onto the stage
how I left a piece of my soul on the creaky uneven floorboards
and whenever I go back the walls whisper my secrets

I float out of my body

watching from beside the ceiling fan

I'd never seen a gun before

I can feel my catholic school teachers fainting somewhere

"what are you gonna do with it"

weightless

my fingertips drain of blood

he smirks:

"relax, it's a prop"

It is

but my stomach continues to sink

I become acutely aware of my sixteenth birthday in this moment

and how I had received a car with a big red bow.

just before the tears blur over my eyes

a laugh escapes my chapped lips

i laugh and laugh at how absurdly horrific it is for one person to have such control

over whether my days will be filled with sun

or called off altogether

due to the tornado warning up ahead.

Whenever I see a candid photograph of myself my breath suspends, almost instantly. I notice my smile never quite reaches my eyes. I am curious by this, almost frightened. I think the camera taunts at me sometimes; a traitor to my best-kept secret. Reminding me at any moment it can reveal what I thought I'd covered up. Only maybe it wasn't a secret at all. I can't tell anymore. My friend reassures me it has something to do with my porcelain skin. "It's not your face. It's the stories men have written about your face." I don't really know what that means, but it must be true because apparently her sister has the same thing.

We pretend between the sheets.

Pretend it means less. Pretend it means more.

up on the rooftop
with our bare feet
dangling we talked
about whether we
thought God was
really out there and
I finally confessed
my hideous middle
name and we were
convinced we had
figured out what the
hell existed at the
bottom of the ocean
and the planets spun
around us and
breathing felt a
little easier

the night we
exchanged oxygen.

help yourself

to the many masks I can put on for you

tell me who you'd like to see today

and I will do my best to morph my features into her face.

I am completely fascinated as I watch this couple
who have been married for thirty-one years
do seemingly mindless tasks

shuffling around the kitchen in their slippers
so in sync to each other's rhythms
so familiar with how the other operates

there is an ease in navigating space

I wonder what that must feel like
to know another human being so completely
in all phases of life
their habits
their movements
their neurosis
their imperfections
what turns them on
what makes them crazy
what secrets they hold

watching them dance around like that gutted me
I thanked them for dinner as I fumbled to button up my fuzzy purple coat

what if no one ever knows me?

I wasn't really hungry

I wasn't really anything

and maybe that was the problem.

even as it was happening I knew I couldn't keep it up
how could I sustain this way of living
when even during the highest peaks,
I could feel my ribcage crack
pulling at me to come back down.

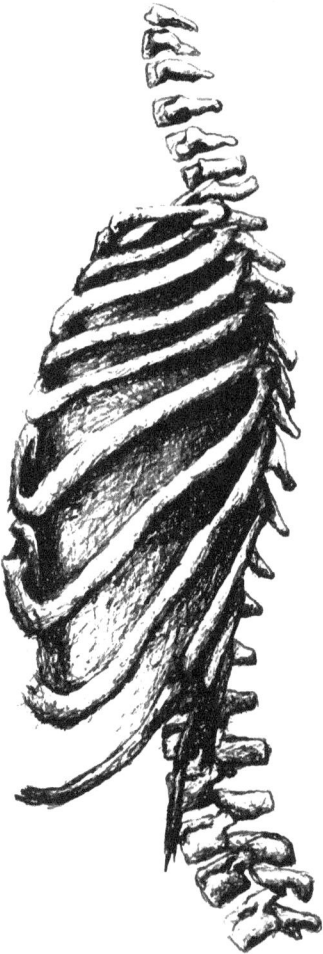

I suddenly had a very overwhelming feeling that the world was all too much.

in the crowd of men

whose hands were too low on my back

between the pulse of the music, and the taste of cheap liquor

my head spun off my neck

he didn't speak a word of english

but bodies talk

I can't possibly be the only girl to realize in the morning light I've changed my mind.

Oh hush, we all love a good train wreck

as long as we're watching from far enough away.

Of all the things I could say about him :

what eats away at me during sleepless nights

is what does it say about me,

and the fact that I stayed.

It was like a sickness I couldn't cover up anymore. It all rolled off my tongue so effortlessly, the words rapidly tumbling out of my fingertips.

I was finally free.

today you fucked me as if I was faceless
like I could have been anyone
I try to recall the days we locked eyes
the days we connected -
the days you were gentle.
I'm pretty sure we hate each other (my third eye seems to know so)
but then you kiss the tip of my nose
that way you used to
and I forget to double check.

the sticky layer that coats my skin, that has now become my safety pin
is screaming at me to run and wash October off
but my blinders are on too thick, and my back can't seem to bend that way
so I move and morph around it as my tongue begins to tangle
guarding the words "we've curdled" to escape from my sticky lips.

that love gloss in your eyes
that used to liquify my limbs and burst the butterflies in my chest
now stings into my collection of tinfoil cuts.
I am locked out of my fantasy haze
it pushes against the backs of my teeth, lapping me up like liquid sugar
swallowing me whole
I am not ready
Can you not see that my pixelated pieces are drenched in your crimson shadow?
Can you not fetch me a towel, to mop up the shame that is dripping down my thighs -
the shame that is now pooling at my feet.

I watched you zip up your duffle bag
and ask me one last time if I couldn't just forgive you
I heard your fist go through the hallway on your way out

Later I found your navy t-shirt
wrapped up beneath the bed sheets
hiding from our madness

Please come back because I have your t-shirt

It smelt like you
and all I could do was clutch my hand over my heart
terrified if I moved it might fall right out

I pictured calling my mother to come put it back inside me
"I told you this would happen, didn't I?" she'd say, relishing in the flames of it all.
"You should never trust anyone whose father lives in prison."

You said I appear often   as pixelated images

trapped inside your brain

i awoke, sweating feverishly

i dreamt you had killed me :

wrung my neck with your calloused hands, licked my frigid blood from your fingerprints

you stirred - "bad dream?"

i ignored my pleading subconscious, swallowing the familiar knot

that accompanied my voracious appetite to please you.

I feel the color grey today

sludgy

ashy

not quite sinking into the depths of my blacks

certainly too afraid to bathe in my whites

so there I stay

grey

grey

grey

praying the storm will pass

transforming me into the lavish lavender I always thought I ought to be.

it hurts to swallow today

i don't really know why i don't want to sleep. my
insides are all twisted and i can't find the calm. i
refuse to slide into a nothing state. it
makes me sad or something.

I wondered if any of these thoughts were even mine...

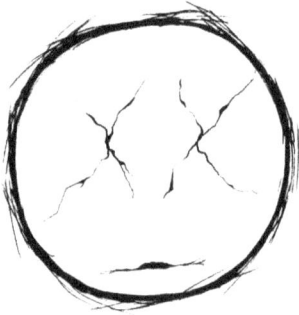

I click refresh to connect

I click

I click

I click

my battery drains

and so do i

I miss the waves of inconsistency I so desperately settled for.

a knot you now realize you let them tie

if you aren't careful

next it will be your noose

he made it a rule that anytime i was upset, i had to sit on his lap with my legs wrapped around his torso and explain what was really wrong. he had the kind of patience no one had bothered to have with me before. he was soft and kind and understood how to ease my messy, combative temper. you scoffed at dealing with issues like that, throwing my legs off you and telling me my ex-boyfriend sounded like a pussy. your way of dealing with things was turning off your cell phone and calling in a few days to ask if i was over it yet. my girlfriends joked that all these stories made me sound like the poster child for daddy issues. that would have stung a lot more if i hadn't silently been thinking the same thing.

there is great clarity that comes with being so completely devastated.

"how was your date?"
i immediately felt a flicker of fire in the pit of my stomach as i anxiously awaited your answer

"it was good, she was fun"

"fun like slutty?"

you gave me a look
a look like you knew exactly what i was doing
i felt exposed
ugly
childish
sloppy
but also the uncontrollable urge to keep going

"was she pretty? i heard when she takes off her makeup she kind of looks like a boy"

she didn't and we both knew it
she was beautiful in all the ways i wasn't

you shrugged

"you know, sometimes you can be really mean'"

the seasons change

as I float away

the city can be so chaotic

colors - sounds - energies

people rushing from train to train

walking with such importance

(it can make you feel like you're missing out on something you didn't even know you wanted)

I wondered how many times someone perceived me to be going somewhere significant

when really I was hustling aimlessly

lost like the rest of them.

we were sane in all the ways the others were crazy

my soul often flutters
at the thought of flying off
to exist somewhere new

to belong to something else
someone else

but what if I am trying to escape from
myself?

i smile at a photo you posted

greeted by a flush of rose to my cheeks

the crooked floors of manhattan are just as charming as you are

as you appear

i remind myself i exist only a blink for you

in an apartment

where the plants grow

and nothing else

It's kind of strange, experiencing life with the intention of re-living it:

hoping moments matter more than they should,

looking for things and people and places to move me

All so I can re-create it later when someone tells me to.

I'm just musing out loud

but I think in a past life we were once really happy

and maybe this was all a temporary glitch

but on this plane

and in this lifetime

it's like catching fireflies

and I cannot continue to be a fragile paper doll for you.

so I hope all your colors come back

and your weary soul finally finds a home

that is not bound to mine.

the waves of energy between us pulsed
as my body gravitated towards yours like a sleek silver magnet
i felt a shock surging through my fingertips
as i artfully brushed them over your shoulder blade

it was cold out
and we both knew you and Allie had once been high school sweethearts
but your brown eyes danced under the september sky
and i told myself first loves can be forgotten

my favorite night of that pumpkin summer was when it poured and ruined our plans
I shrieked for shelter and ran toward the deck
you lost one of your sandals in the mud
we never did find it

the rain waltzed with the ocean waves
as we peeled off our clothes, hair dripping onto the kitchen floor
your touch gave me the kind of butterflies I could never catch

this is the image I recall, you unraveling me
whenever I am caught in a rainstorm.

I long for a life I am completely enchanted with.

Lately I've been meeting a lot of Insta-Selfie Contour Queens
bred in bulk by society and then labeled as cashmere
But to me it feels more like those scratchy cotton sweaters you buy on a whim at Kind Exchange
when you're running late and your mother texts you   "Don't forget to bring a jacket!"
These Insta-Selfie Contour Queens fascinate me
the way they have been taught to search your eyes

                                                    to find their reflections
as if moving mouths have suddenly become cameras, and they are determined to find their light.
lost
between the lines of photography
and personality
between
posing and existing   people are so beautiful when they aren't trying to be.
These Insta-Selfie Contour Queens have inspired me to do this thing
this deranged, foreign, rebellious act that now isolates me from 2018's Most Beautiful Creatures
It's this thing where I express my brush strokes
where I actively resist the sweltering pressure to apply black when my insides are screaming neon.
where I claw back at the fashion-forward photoshop that not-so-subtly makes the bridge of my nose
just a little smaller
and my eyes just a little larger
and my lips plumper
and my waist thinner
and my hair longer and my Kim K booty poppin'
strategically leaving my thoughts   and opinions   and ideas
abandoned
like the burden of that extra cost for checked luggage that is ultimately left going 'round and 'round
on the baggage carousel with no one to claim it.
I'm discovering the joy in silencing this static
to proudly blink purple in a sea of sable, regardless if the shade doesn't quite match my complexion.

for even in the depth of night
the shadows always fade come morning.

honey those were some dark days,
but I am determined to exist in the light.

for as long as I can recall
I've had this hole in my soul
after my father died
and the important parts of my mother died along with him
the hole began, drilling itself into my atmosphere.
it is not large
and it does not constantly ache
but it is there
demanding of my attention when left open.

so I became desperate to fill it
with different booze and different boys
like a rolled up paper towel you stuff into a sink
a placeholder
a 'for now'
to make it stop.
eventually, it overflowed
forcing me to sit in the swamp of it all
sit in the swamp that is me.

but what if this time I don't fill it?
what if this time
I pull everything out I've used to stop the bleeding
expose the wound, hope for healing
take a deep breath
and surrender.

as i shed my cracked and bitter skins
i feel a sense of rebirth
an alternate shape forming

if i can stay true to exploring these cold and hollow corners
maybe I can live in a world
where pinky promises mean something again.

we are not any one moment

we are a collection of moments
through a collection of lifetimes

and that is a beautiful gift

for everything I have
for everywhere I've been

and all the places I have yet to go.

one thousand matches

Carly MacIsaac is a Toronto-based artist with an endless curiosity for human behavior, visual storytelling, and emotional connection. She grew up on stage as a theatre actor before pursuing a career in film.

one thousand matches is Carly's debut collection of poetry, reflecting upon the turbulent journey toward self-forgiveness; striking a match to the past, sitting amongst the ashes - and ultimately finding the bravery to rebuild. Carly's work can also be found in *Blank Spaces, Breadcrumbs, Planet S* and her upcoming web-series *Easy V.*

Carly's deepest hope is for others to come across her words and feel less alone because of something they identify with. This book is dedicated to anyone struggling with the seemingly impossible task of overcoming grief, toxic relationships, or an absence of self-worth. Please know it is never too late to grant yourself the beautiful offering of a second chance.

www.carlymacisaac.com
@onethousandmatches

www.ingramcontent.com/pod-product-compliance
Lightning Source LLC
Chambersburg PA
CBHW020604030426
42337CB00013B/1205